marie claire
idées

Paper Crafts with Style

Over 50 Designs Made with Cut, Folded, Pasted, and Stitched Paper

TRAFALGAR SQUARE
North Pomfret, Vermont

First published in the United States of America in 2009 by
Trafalgar Square Books, North Pomfret, Vermont 05053

Printed in China

Original title: Créations en papier
© 2005 by Éditions MARIE CLAIRE–Société d'Information et de Créations (SIC)
10, boulevard des Frères-Voisin,
92130 Issy-Les-Moulineaux Cedex 9 – France

English language text copyright © 2009 Quadrille Publishing Limited
Original design, layout, text, photographs, and artworks copyright © 2009 SIC

Translation and project management: Anne McDowall
Production Director: Vincent Smith
Production Controller: Denise Stone

ISBN: 978-1-57076-427-1

Library of Congress Control Number: 2008937234

10 9 8 7 6 5 4 3 2 1

NOTES
Some of the templates have been reduced in scale. To find their correct size, enlarge them on
a photocopier until the scale bar on the template shows the measurement indicated.

Paper Crafts with Style

Over 50 Designs Made with Cut, Folded, Pasted, and Stitched Paper

Contents

For the table

DECORATIVE PLATES

MATERIALS
Sheets of white letter paper ●
Scissors ● Glass or clear plastic
plates ● Tracing paper ● Spray
adhesive.

METHOD
Cut out circles of paper of the same
diameter as the plates. Fold each
circle into 8. Enlarge the motifs on
page 110 onto tracing paper so that
they are of the same size as the
folded paper circles. Trace the motifs
onto one side of each of the folded
paper cones, then cut out the
designs carefully so that you are left
with only the white areas. Unfold the
paper decorations.

Working on a newspaper-covered
surface and in a well-ventilated area,
adhere the paper decorations onto
the underside of the plates using
spray adhesive. Make sure that the
smallest pieces are well secured so
that they don't become unstuck
and crinkled.

(Note: these plates are purely
decorative and cannot be placed in
the dishwasher.)

(see also page 110)

For the table

CUTLERY MENU
Size: 9⅝ x 4¾ in

MATERIALS

Cardstock for the menus ● Craft knife ● Metal ruler ● Colored tracing paper ● India ink and pen ● Spray adhesive ● Buttons ● Glue stick ● Colored thread.

METHOD

Cut 9⅝ in squares of cardstock for the menus and fold them in half. Using the ruler, tear along the vertical edges of the cardstock to create a raw unfinished look. Cut rectangles of tracing paper approximately 8⅜ x 3⅝ in for the front of the menus. Reduce the motifs opposite, then place the tracing paper rectangles on top and trace the design in India ink.

Stick a tracing paper rectangle onto the front of each menu card using spray adhesive. Attach a button onto the front of the menu using the glue stick. Make a loop from colored thread and glue the ends onto the back of the card, opposite the button, to form a button loop.

2 in

- Menu -

For the table

NEWSPAPER DISHES

MATERIALS
Dishes (to serve as molds) ● **Petroleum jelly** ● **Bowl** ● **White glue** ● **Sheets of newspaper** ● **Glue brush** ● **Scissors** ● **Gray acrylic paint** ● **Paintbrush.**

METHOD
Cover the inside of the mold with petroleum jelly. In a bowl, mix some white glue with water to thin it slightly. Tear the newspaper into small strips, coat them with glue, then stick them over the inside of the mold in an even layer. Leave to dry completely before applying the second layer. You will need at least 5 layers of paper to create a firm dish. For a pleasing effect, use pieces of paper with the same size type for the final layer.
When the dish is completely dry, remove the mold and trim the edges of the dish with scissors. Paint a thin and a slightly thicker line around the inner edge using gray acrylic paint. The dried glue will form a protective varnish.

For the table

FAIRY TEA SERVICE

MATERIALS

Teapot and cup (to serve as molds) ● Plastic wrap ● Red and plum-colored tissue paper ● Bowl ● White glue ● Glue brush ● Wire ● Strong glue (for attaching wire handles) ● Craft knife.

METHOD

Cover the teapot and cup with plastic wrap, pulling it tight to avoid wrinkles. Tear the tissue paper into small pieces. In a bowl, mix some white glue with water to thin it slightly. Cover the pieces of tissue paper with glue and apply them to the plastic wrap-covered surfaces using the glue brush.

Cup: Cover the outer surface of the cup with glued tissue paper. Leave to dry completely, then add another layer. Once this layer is dry, carefully remove the mold and plastic wrap. Cover the inside of the cup with pieces of glued paper, using the same technique, and leaving each layer to dry thoroughly before applying the next one, until the cup is firm enough.

Cut a length of wire, twist it into a handle, and attach it to the side of the cup using strong glue.

Teapot: Cover the whole surface of the teapot with pieces of glued tissue paper. Leave to dry, then apply a second layer.

Once this is completely dry, carefully split open the papier mâché casing, from top to bottom and through the spout, using a craft knife, to remove the teapot. Place the 2 halves side by side and join them together with a layer of glued paper overlapping the 2 halves.

Finish by making and attaching a wire handle, as for the cup.

For the table

WINDOW AND CAKE GARLANDS

WINDOW GARLAND

MATERIALS
4 sheets of letter-size tracing paper ● Masking tape ● Pencil ● Craft knife ● Card punch ● Cutting mat ● 24 x 20 in of tarlatan ● Scissors ● String ● Glue.

METHOD
Enlarge each of the letter motifs on page 111 to fit on a sheet of tracing paper, then attach them using masking tape. Lightly trace the design onto the tracing paper, then remove the template. Cut out the center of the letters and the other elements in the design.
Cut pieces of tarlatan slightly smaller than the sheets of tracing paper and stick them behind each "empty space."
Cut the string to the required length of the garland and center the letters along it, spacing them about 4 in apart. Fold the top edge over the string and glue in place.

CAKE GARLAND

MATERIALS
Bristol board ● Masking tape ● Craft knife ● Cutting mat.

METHOD
Enlarge the template on page 111 (the size given is for a 4¾–5⅝ in-diameter cake) and attach it to the Bristol board with masking tape. Cut out the outline using a craft knife and cut open the slits. Fold up the edges and slot the tabs into the slits as shown on the template. You can experiment with different sizes of pan and by varying the decoration of the edge.

(see also page 111)

For the table

NOSTALGIA IN GLASS

MATERIALS
Antique glass flycatcher or other glass vessel with a wide mouth ● Flower and foliage découpage motifs ● Nail scissors ● Découpage glue ● Soft cloth ● Clear varnish ● Flexible paintbrush for the varnish ● Fine paintbrush for the paint ● Gloss paint.

1. Carefully cut out the chosen découpage motifs, reserving the more compact flower and foliage pieces for the base of the glass.

2. Coat the printed sides of the designs with glue. Stick them firmly on the interior surface of the jar and press with a soft cloth to remove all air bubbles. Leave to dry.

3. Using a flexible paintbrush, paint over the edges of the designs with a varnish to waterproof the surface. Leave to dry.

4. To finish, fill in the background with gloss paint, using a fine paintbrush, making sure to trace carefully around the motifs.

For the table

LACY MENUS

MATERIALS
Decorative paints ● Paintbrush ●
White or colored blank cards ●
White and gold paper doilies ●
Spray adhesive ● Gold pen ●
Scissors ● Tracing paper ● Gold
metallic elastic cord.

METHOD
Paint the cards and/or the doilies
in your desired colors. Leave to dry.
Cover the cards with the doilies,
inside and out, matching or
contrasting colors. Use spray
adhesive to stick the doilies in place,
folding over excess onto the other
side of the card.
Use a gold pen to highlight details
of the doily pattern and to write
"menu" at the top of each card.
Cut a sheet of tracing paper to the
dimensions of the open card, fold in
half, and slip it inside the card.
Tie a length of gold elastic cord in
place around the spine to hold the
menu in place.

For the table

TIERED TRAY

Size: 20 x 18⅜ in

MATERIALS

3 squares of ¼ in-thick plywood: 18 in², 12⅜ in² and 7¼ in² ● ⅜ in² wooden lath: 4 lengths of 20¾ in, 4 lengths of 17¼ in, 4 lengths of 11⅝ in and 4 lengths of 6⅜ in ● Saw ● Wood glue ● Hammer ● ¾ in-wide finish nails ● Pencil ● Colored tissue paper ● Scissors ● Red and white acrylic paints.

METHOD

Following the diagram opposite, make 2 ladders, joining the lengths of wooden lath together using wood glue and finish nails. Leave to dry. Join the remaining lengths of lath onto 2 top opposite edges of each plywood square using wood glue and finish nails. Leave to dry. Assemble the 2 ladders and 3 trays, gluing and nailing the crosspieces of the ladders to the top of opposite sides of each tray (You will need to cut in to the crosspieces to match them up with the uprights.) Leave to dry. Paint the whole structure using white acrylic paint, then, when dry,

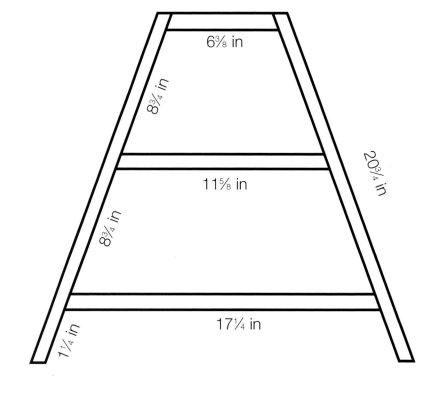

with red acrylic paint. Copy a mosaic design from a book, or make up your own, and draw it lightly onto the tray. Cut out small shapes from

tissue paper and stick them onto the design with diluted wood glue, leaving a gap of about ¼ in between the pieces. Leave to dry.

For the table

DAILY PAPERS

MATERIALS
Table and chairs ● Wallpaper paste ● Bowl ● A large quantity of newspaper ● Paintbrushes ● Wallpaper paste brush ● Matte varnish.

METHOD
Clean the table and chairs to remove any traces of dust or grease that would prevent the newspaper from sticking to them.

Prepare the wallpaper paste in a bowl, following the manufacturer's instructions.

Wet newspaper is fragile to handle, so it is best to work on a small area at a time. Cover the surface to be papered with wallpaper paste, lay a piece of newspaper onto it, and use a paintbrush, coated with more wallpaper paste, to adhere it in place. Use a wallpaper brush to dab the paper around the curves and edges of the table and chairs, making sure that it is pressed into all the corners. Depending on the effect you are wanting to achieve, you can cover each piece of furniture with a single layer of paper or with several, but leave each one to dry before applying the next. Avoid papering the edges of drawers, otherwise the thickness of paper might prevent them from opening, and ensure that the table top is completely flat so that anything you place on it remains stable.

Once the final layer is completely dry, make sure that there are no loose corners of paper peeling up, then apply 2 coats of matte varnish to protect the surfaces.

For the table

ORIGAMI POCKETS

MATERIALS

Colored cardstock: squares of 7¾, 10, 14 and 18 in ● 10 in length of ribbon for each holder ● Tapestry needle ● Gel glue.

METHOD

All these "pockets" are folded in the same way, by marking the folds with your nail at each stage.

Following the diagrams on page 112, fold each square in 4 to mark the center point, then open out again (1). Fold over each corner to the center point (2 and 3). Turn the cardstock over and mark the center as in step 1 (4). Fold the new corners into the center (5). Fold this square in half, from top to bottom (6).

Slide the thumb and index finger of your right hand underneath the righthand corners of the fold (thumb in front, index finger behind); slide the thumb and index finger of your left hand under the lefthand points. Open the pockets by bringing the 4 points to the center. Remove your fingers and thumbs and turn the shape over so that it rests on these 4 points.

Pierce the center of each origami shape and, using the needle, thread through a length of ribbon so that the ends are on the wrong side. Knot the ends and fix them in place with a dab of glue.

Fill the pockets with rose petals, little pebbles, sweets, salt, or pepper...

(see also page 112)

Vases and flowers

TALL RED VASES

MATERIALS

Muslin ● Iron-on interfacing ● Scissors ● Needle ● Sewing thread ● Bowl ● White glue ● Glue brush ● Red tissue paper and/or Chinese paper.

METHOD

In the muslin and interfacing, cut a 4 in-diameter circle and a rectangle of 13¼ in x the desired height of the vase, adding a ⅜ in seam allowance around all sides. Iron the interfacing onto each piece.

Make the rectangle into a tube by sewing together the 2 heights, right sides together, then sew the tube around the circle. Turn right side out. In a bowl, mix some white glue with water to thin it slightly. Tear the tissue paper and/or Chinese paper into small pieces. Coat the paper with glue and apply it to the tube, working from the bottom up. Allow each layer to dry before applying the next one. When the final layer is completely dry, even up the top edge with scissors.

Vases and flowers

WEDDING POSY

MATERIALS
White, lilac, and pale green tissue paper ● Scissors ● Thick white cotton thread ● Toothpicks.

METHOD
For each flower stem, cut a 31½ x ¾ in strip of green tissue paper and a 31½ in length of cotton thread. Lay the thread along one long edge of the paper and, with wet fingers, roll the paper around it. Leave to dry. For each petal, cut a 8 x 2 in strip of tissue paper. Lay a toothpick at an angle across one of the short edges (see opposite), then roll the paper around it until you reach the center. Do the same from the other top corner. Carefully remove the toothpicks. Prepare other petals in the same way. To make different sizes of flower, allow between 5 and 20 petals for each one.

Curl one end of a dried stem to form a stamen, then lay it across the base of a petal so it overlaps the petal edge by about 2⅜ in. With wet fingers, roll the base of the petal around the stem. Fix all the petals to the stem in the same way.

Vases and flowers

EXOTIC STAMP VASE

MATERIALS
A large quantity of floral stamps (or printouts or photocopies of stamp motifs) ● Vase ● Strong glue ● Glue brush ● Yellow and sepia ink ● Paintbrushes (for inks and varnish) ● Antiquing varnish.

METHOD
Sort the stamps according to their format so that you can easily select the best ones to use on different parts of the vase. Stick them to the vase with strong glue, overlapping them so that none of the vase can be seen. Leave to dry.
Mix the inks in equal quantities and paint over the stamps. Leave to dry, then paint the vase with antiquing varnish to protect and antiquate it.

Vases and flowers

FLOWER BAG

MATERIALS

Strong cardstock gift bag ● Sharp pencil ● Sewing machine ● Colored sewing thread ● Paper glue ● Thin wire ● Small colored beads ● Card punch ● Cutting mat ● 4 eyelets, ¼ in wide ● Eyelet setter ● Hammer.

METHOD

Remove the handles from the bag and carefully unglue the seams so that you can lay it flat.

Draw the design onto the bag with a pencil. Thread the sewing machine with colored thread and machine-stitch over the design using a satin stitch of width ⅔ and length 0.5.

Reassemble the bag, gluing the seams with paper glue.

Cut a length of thin wire for each handle and thread the beads onto these wires.

Make 2 holes on each side of the bag, spacing them equidistant from each side. Push the eyelet through the punched-out hole. Have the decorative side of the eyelet face down toward the cutting mat, with the fastener side facing up toward you. Place the tip of the eyelet setter into the center of the fastener. With a hammer, tap the top of the eyelet setter. Remove the eyelet setter. Using the hammer, tap down the edges of the fastener to flatten to the bag.

Slip the ends of one handle into the 2 holes in the front of the bag, the ends of the other handle into those in the back. Twist the ends on the wrong side to secure the handles in place. Reshape the handles.

Vases and flowers

FOLDED PAPER VASES

MATERIALS
Stiff cardstock ● Scissors ● Cylindrical vase ● Pencil ● Ruler ● Round coffee filter papers ● Sewing machine ● White sewing thread ● Strong glue.

METHOD
Cut a rectangle of cardstock to cover the vase, allowing an extra strip for the overlap. Using the pencil and ruler, divide the rectangle into horizontal bands the same height as the diameter of the filter papers. Then draw vertical lines ⅜ in apart, staggering the rows from one horizontal band to the next.

Fold the filter papers in half and stitch them onto the cardstock, placing the center fold of a filter paper against each of the vertical pencil lines, to completely cover the surface of the card.

Wrap the card around the vase and glue in place.

Vases and flowers

POTS OF FLOWERS

MATERIALS

Compost pots ● White acrylic paint ● Paintbrush ● Thin wire ● Pliers ● Scissors ● Tissue paper: pink, white, mauve, and red ● All-purpose glue.

METHOD

Paint the compost pots with a thin layer of white acrylic paint.

For each of the small roses and rosebuds, cut a 10 in length of wire. Fold the wire in half and twist the ends together, leaving a small loop at the center.

For each of the large roses, cut a 20 in length of wire. Leaving 4¾ in at each end, twist the central part to make about 10 heart-shaped petals of different sizes, their bases all joining in the center. Twist the ends of the wire together.

Cut hearts of various sizes from the tissue paper. Paint one side of each heart white, experimenting with different intensities of color.

For the small roses, glue a petal to each side of the wire loop, then glue the bases of 10 others all around the twisted-wire stem.

For the large roses, group petals all around the stem and between the wire petals, gluing their bases to the twisted wire.

Arrange the flowers in the compost pots, mixing up the sizes and colors, then place the pots down the center of the table.

Vases and flowers

PAPIER MÂCHÉ JUGS

MATERIALS

Brass wire ● Wire cutters ● 1 in-diameter wire mesh ● Flat-nosed pliers ● Bowl ● Large quantity of newspaper ● White and colored acrylic paints ● Paintbrushes.

METHOD

You will need to build a wire structure for each of the jugs. Using the brass wire, form a ring for the base, one for the top—adding a lip—and several intermediate ones. Working from the bottom to the top, join the rings together with at least 8 vertical wires, attaching the latter to the rings with knots of brass wire. Add handles, and spouts to the jug forms, and construct the shape for the teapot lid, as desired.

To create an armature (the skeleton), wrap the mesh over the structural frame. Fold in edges over the wire structure and tie with brass wires as needed.

Tear the newspaper into strips, and prepare the wallpaper paste in a bowl, following the manufacturer's instructions. Coat the newspaper strips with wallpaper paste, then lay them onto the structure, overlapping them slightly to cover the whole surface. Leave to dry. Add several layers, leaving each to dry before applying the next, until the shapes are generously covered and suitably robust.

Apply several coats of white paint to the jugs to give a uniform color, leave to dry, then paint each in coordinating or contrasting colors of your choice.

Vases and flowers

ARUM-LILY CORONET

MATERIALS

Tracing paper ● Pencil ● White paper ● Scissors ● Sheets of newspaper ● Paper glue ● Paintbrushes ● Acrylic paints: white, golden yellow, pistachio green, and pale spring green ● Hairdryer ● Wallpaper paste ● Bowl ● 6 yds of ¹⁄₁₀ in-diameter wire ● Cutting pliers ● Nylon thread ● Needle.

METHOD

Trace the motifs on page 113 and cut them out to make a template. Cut out 9 flowers and 12 leaves in the white paper.

Cut a 4 x 2 in strip of newspaper for each flower and leaf. Roll up each strip tightly from the short side, securing at the end with a line of glue, to make a 2 in-long stick.

Roll the leaves and flowers around these "stamens" as shown in the diagrams on page 113, securing them in place by gluing a little ring of paper tightly around the base.

Paint the flowers and leaves with at least 5 coats of white paint, drying them with a hairdryer between each one. (These layers of paint will help to solidify the elements.) Paint the leaves in the shades of green and the stamens in golden yellow. Leave to dry.

Tear the remaining newspaper into strips and prepare the wallpaper paste in a bowl, following the manufacturer's instructions. Coat the newspaper strips with wallpaper paste and wrap them tightly around the wire. Leave to dry.

Paint with white acrylic paint, then, when dry, with green. Curl the wire into a coronet about 24 in in diameter. To complete the coronet, sew the leaves and flowers onto it using the nylon thread.

(see also page 113)

Vases and flowers

BOUQUET OF FLOWERS

MATERIALS

Pencil ● Compass ● White tissue paper ● Scissors ● Thin wire ● Round black sticky labels.

METHOD

Using a pencil, and a compass if necessary, trace the circles on page 114 directly onto sheets of white tissue paper, lightly marking the parts to be cut out—shown in gray on the template. (Alternatively, you can simply draw circles of approximately 3⅝ in diameter and cut out different designs freehand.) Cut out the circles, fold in half, then in half again, then into 3, keeping the segment with the design drawn on it on top. Cutting through all layers of paper at once, remove the marked parts of the design. Open out the circles.

Cut the flower stems from the thin wire and poke one end through the center of each flower, from back to front. Bend over the wire end and stick a black label on top to hide it and form the flower center.

(see also page 114)

Lights

PUNCHED HOLES

DECORATIVE VOTIVES

MATERIALS
Glass tumblers ● Scrap paper ● Handmade paper ● Scissors ● Large needle ● Strong glue.

METHOD
Wrap a tumbler in a piece of paper to obtain its dimensions. Transfer the shape to a sheet of handmade paper, allowing an extra strip for the overlap. Cut out this pattern.
Enlarge the motifs on page 115 on a photocopier so that they fit the size of the tumblers. Place them on the paper and, working on a protected surface, punch the holes using a large needle. Glue the hole-punched paper around the glass.
Take inspiration from these 3 motifs and design your own decorative ones. (Search through cross-stitch books to discover lots of frieze and festive design ideas.)

SMALL DISHES

MATERIALS
Sheets of newspaper ● Bowl ● Electric mixer ● 2 sieves of the same size ● White and gold acrylic paint ● 1 large and 1 medium paintbrush.

METHOD
Tear the newspaper into tiny pieces and leave to soak overnight in a bowl of water. Squeeze out excess water, then blend the soaked paper in the mixer to form a thick pulp.
Spread around the base and sides of one of the sieves to a thickness of about ¼ in. Press the other sieve inside and leave to dry.
Remove the hardened dish from the mould and paint the inside and outside using white acrylic paint. Paint the rim of the dish gold.

(see also page 115)

Lights

PAPER PUMPKINS

MATERIALS

Newspaper ● Garland of white Japanese lanterns ● Colored stickers: 2 sizes of round stickers and 2 sizes of stars ● Rubber gloves ● Orange spray paint ● Spool of wire ● Wire cutters ● Japanese paper: 1 sheet of dark green and 1 sheet of medium green ● Pencil ● Spray adhesive ● Eraser ● Scissors.

METHOD

Working in a well-ventilated but draft-free space, and on a newspaper-covered surface, re-form the lanterns, remove them from the garland, and decorate with stickers. Wearing rubber gloves, cover the lanterns with a light but even coat of orange spray paint. Leave to dry, then spray with a second coat to ensure that the color is as uniform as possible.

Cut some 3 in lengths of wire. Apply glue to one side of the medium-green paper and wrap the paper around the wires. Twist the wires around a finger or a pencil to form tendrils.

Trace the leaf shape below and transfer it to the dark-green paper. Tear or cut out several leaves. Spray adhesive to the bottom of the strips and attach them to the wire stems.

When the painted lanterns are completely dry, carefully remove the stickers. Attach the wire stems to the structure of the lanterns, then reattach these to the garland.

Template to scale

Lights

CURLED-PAPER LAMPSHADE

MATERIALS

2 sheets of textured white cardstock, each 40 x 27½ in ● Pencil ● Ruler ● Craft knife ● 1 lampshade frame: 10/12 in in diameter, 11⅝ in high ● Glue gun.

METHOD

Cut the cardstock into 27½ x 1¼ in strips. Curl one end to 8 in of its length. Turn the strip over and repeat with the other end.

Position the curled strips on the lampshade frame by folding them over the top rim by varying amounts to give strips of different lengths, some with curls facing outward, with others facing inward. Glue them in position using the glue gun. If necessary, you can fill any gaps with strips that have been rolled at only one end.

Lights

FLORAL SHADES

MATERIALS

White and orange recycled paper ● Scissors ● Paper glue ● Craft knife ● Cutting mat ● Pencil or crayons ● Eraser ● ¼ in-diameter wooden dowel ● Long wooden skewers.

METHOD

Cut squares or rectangles of paper of adequate size to screen your chosen lights.

Draw daisies on the paper with the pencil or crayons (the latter if you want to retain these marks as part of the design). Carefully cut out certain parts of the flowers using the craft knife.

For a flat screen (as top right), cut the wooden dowel to the lengths of the sides and glue to the edges on the back to form a frame.

To make the curved screens, pierce the middle of each side edge with a wooden skewer that is shorter than the width of the paper. Secure with dabs of glue on the inside. (If the screen is large, use 2 skewers across the top and bottom.)

Lights

SUMMER LANTERN

MATERIALS

White decorative paper ● Straight-sided glass vase ● Scissors ● Craft knife ● Multi-surface 3D paint ● Paintbrush ● Hairdryer (optional, see method) ● Strong glue ● Pencil ● White handmade paper ● Thin twig ● String of mini Christmas lights.

METHOD

Cut a rectangle of the decorative paper the height of your vase and long enough to encircle it, allowing for an overlap to glue it in place.

The design of the paper used for this lantern has holes with raised edges. If you are unable to find something similar, cut out irregular circles over the whole surface using a craft knife and paint a fine line of multi-surface 3D paint around each hole. Dry the paint with a hairdryer to puff up the paint.

Stick the paper around the vase with a line of glue on the overlapping edge.

Draw a large butterfly freehand on the white handmade paper and cut out. Stick it onto the top of the twig, then slide the other end of the twig through a hole in the lantern.

Feed the mini lights into the vase, hiding the cord at the back.

Lights

NEWSPRINT LANTERNS
Sizes: 6 x 4 in and 8 x 6 in

MATERIALS
⅛ in-thick cardboard (see method for dimensions) ● Craft knife ● ⅜ in-square wooden rod (allow 1.1 yds length for small lantern and 1.6 yds for large one) ● Pencil ● Ruler ● Saw ● Glue gun ● Old foreign newspapers ● Scissors ● Tealights ● Glass votives.

METHOD
For the small lantern, cut a 4 in square of the ⅛ in-thick cardboard to form the base. Cut 4 lengths of wooden rod of 6 in to form the uprights of the structure. Using the glue gun, glue the ends to each of the corners of the base.

Cut 4 lengths of rod of 3¼ in and glue them between the uprights at the top to strengthen and complete the structure.

Once the glue is completely dry, cover the structure with strips of newspaper, either using one large piece and wrapping and gluing it tightly around the whole structure, or covering each side with a rectangle of paper. Leave to dry.

Make the large lantern in the same way, using a 2⅜ in cardboard square for the base, 8 in lengths of rod for the uprights and 6 in-long rods for the top of the frame.

Place a tealight in a glass votive into the bottom of each of the lanterns.

Lights

CANDELABRA
Size: 23¼ x 33⅝ in

MATERIALS
3 mm-thick grayboard: 2 sheets of 47¼ x 32 in ● Scissors ● Craft knife ● Protractor ● Pencil ● White glue ● Elastic band ● Rope ● Tarlatan ● Newspaper ● Bowl ● Wallpaper paste ● Tissue paper ● Paintbrushes ● Gray acrylic paint ● Thick long needle ● Wire ● Wire cutters ● 6 tealights .

METHOD
Enlarge the template on page 116 and, using a craft knife, cut out 6 candelabra shapes with arms and 6 without (following the dotted line) from the grayboard. Cut out a 9¼ in-diameter circle for the base of the candelabra. On the base of this circle, draw 6 diameters to divide it into 12 segments of equal size.
Draw a line of white glue along each radius of the circle, then place the bottom edge of the candelabra shapes onto them, alternating shapes with and without arms, so that the shapes all join in the center. Hold the shapes together while the glue dries with an elastic band around the body of the candelabra. Cut 12 reinforcing pieces—shown in gray on the template—from the grayboard. Stick them on both sides of each arm. Cut out 36 half-candle-ring shapes and 6 circles of 4 in in diameter. Stick the flat sides of 3 half-candle-ring shapes to each side of the candle-ring at the end of each arm, spacing them at equal angles apart. Stick one of the card circles on top of each candle-ring. Knot one end of the rope and lay it so the knot lies just below the neck and between two segments of the candelabra. Carefully tape the rope to each side of the segment for added security.
Cut strips of tarlatan about 1¼ in wide and wrap them around the candelabra, attaching them in place with a few spots of glue.
In a bowl, mix up the wallpaper paste, following the manufacturer's instructions. Tear up the newspaper into strips, soak in the wallpaper paste, and apply to the candelabra shape. Allow each layer to dry before applying the next one. Finish with a layer of tissue paper. Once the candelabra is completely dry, paint it using gray acrylic paint. Place a tealight on each candle-ring and suspend the candelabra from the ceiling with the rope.

(see also page 116)

Lights

FEATHERED PAPER LANTERN

MATERIALS

**White and pink acrylic paints ●
Small jars or plastic cups for
mixing paint ● Paper lantern ●
Paintbrush ● White glue ● Pink
feathers.**

METHOD

Put some white acrylic paint in each
of several jars or cups. Add some
pink paint to each cup, varying the
amount added to each cup to give
different shades of pink.

Paint each section of the paper
lampshade in a different shade of
pink. (Note: the paint will need to
be relatively thick to prevent it
soaking the paper.) Leave to dry.

Glue the feathers onto the
lampshade in a random pattern.

Lights

CHINESE LANTERNS
Size: 12 x 8 in

MATERIALS
Transparent self-adhesive vinyl contact paper (you will need a 32¾ x 12 in rectangle for each lantern) ● Ruler ● Pencil ● Scissors ● Tissue paper in various bright colors ● Craft knife ● Thin wooden rod (you will need a 1¾ yds length for each rectangular lantern) ● Rubber cement ● 8 in-diameter wire lampshade frame ● Thin wire ● Needle ● Colored paper ● Spray adhesive.

METHOD
Cut an 32¾ x 12 in rectangle from the transparent self-adhesive vinyl contact paper. Mark ⅜ in in from both sides of the long edge. Between these 2 points, mark 3 lines at 8 in intervals along the length for the lantern corners (see the diagram on page 117). Remove the backing paper and carefully lay tissue paper over the surface, leaving ⅜ in at each short edge clear. Press in place.

Cut 8 lengths of wooden rod of 7¾ in and glue them along each long side, as shown on page 117, using rubber cement. Form the lantern by sticking the two short edges together on the inside.

Slip the lampshade frame into the top of the lantern. Secure it in position with several stitches of wire through the vinyl contact paper.

Cut out various motifs—starfish, shells, or birds, for example—from the colored paper. Stick them onto each side of the lantern using the spray adhesive.

Make various lanterns in the same way, varying the colors, decoration, and dimensions as desired (making sure that you can find lampshade frames of a suitable size to fit).

(see also page 117)

Lights

TEALIGHT HOLDERS

MATERIALS

4 glass votives ● Japanese handmade paper ● Scissors ● 3D craft paint ● Letter stencils ● Stencil brush ● Paper glue ● 4 tealights.

METHOD

Cut out 4 strips from the Japanese paper the height of the votives and long enough to encircle the them and allow for an overlap of ¾ in.

Lay a letter stencil in the middle of each paper strip and apply the 3D craft paint using a stencil brush. Leave the paint to dry before removing the stencil.

Close the bands with a few dabs of glue along the edge. Slip them over the glass votives and place a tealight in each one. **(As a safety precaution, make sure that the paper band is no higher than the top of the votives.)**

Gift wrapping

QUILLED-PAPER BOXES

MATERIALS

**White card boxes with lids ●
Decorative paints ● Small paint
roller ● Thick paper of different
colors ● Craft knife ● Small metal
ruler ● All-purpose glue ● Knitting
needle or pencil ● Toothpick ●
Tweezers.**

METHOD

Paint the outside of each box and
its lid, using the roller, with 2 coats
of paint, leaving the paint to dry
after each coat.

Cut strips of colored paper ⅛–¼ in
wide. For the linear motifs, such as
the letters or flower stems shown
opposite, design the chosen shapes
onto the box using a pencil or end
of a knitting needle. Use a toothpick
to trace a line of glue in the channel
thus formed, then carefully place
the paper strips into position, laying
them flat or on their sides,
depending on the effect desired.

Shape relief motifs, such as the
clovers and hearts, from the paper
strips by rolling the ends around the
knitting needle to create scrolls.
Using the toothpick, carefully draw
a line of glue along the edge of the
curled strips and place them into
position on the boxes, holding them
in place for a minute with your
finger. You can use tweezers to
handle the smallest motifs.

Gift wrapping

FANTASTIC BOXES

MATERIALS
Old boxes ● An assortment of colored papers: candy wrappers, paper doilies, foreign packaging, stickers, papers with different textures, shredded tissue paper ● Paper glue ● Gloss medium or clear varnish ● Paintbrush.

METHOD
Cover the boxes in different papers, overlapping them to cover all surfaces. Smooth out bubbles and wrinkles using your thumb, being careful not to rip the paper. Apply 3 or 4 coats of gloss medium or clear varnish to the finished surface after it has completely dried. Allow the surface to dry between coats.

Alternatively, wrap a box in colored paper, then attach pieces of other papers or stickers.

The wild box in the top left corner of the picture is covered with strips of tissue paper that have been passed through a paper shredder.

Gift wrapping

CUT-PAPER COVERINGS

MATERIALS

Large sheets of thick white paper ● Cutting mat ● Pencil ● Craft knife ● Paper glue ● Colored tissue paper ● Textured white wallpaper ● Foreign newspapers.

METHOD

To make the paper cornet, spread out a sheet of paper on the cutting mat. Sketch motifs in pencil onto the paper: draw the geometric motifs on the wrong side, any text or letters on the right side. Carefully cut out the shapes using the craft knife. Roll the paper into a cone shape, gluing it in place. Slip a sheet of colored tissue paper inside the paper cornet to highlight the cut-out motifs.

To make the raised-flower wrapping paper (as used on three boxes and the bag on the chair), cut a piece of the textured white paper large enough to wrap the present. Mark the part that will cover the top of the parcel. Working slowly and carefully, cut the outline of flower shapes, making sure that you always leave a part to attach the flower to the paper. Wrap up the present in the paper, then, using a craft knife, carefully lift the cut pieces away from the rest.

To make the tousled flowers, cut a long strip of white paper or foreign newpaper. Draw a line $3/8$ in in from the edge along the length of this strip, then cut from the edge to this line every $1/4$ or $1/2$ in. Roll up the strip and glue the loose end. Stick it onto the package, then separate the "petals."

Gift wrapping

MONEY-COVERED BOXES

MATERIALS

1 wooden wine crate (with lid) and 1 tea caddy or cigar box ● A large quantity of paper money and coins ● Sandpaper ● Spray adhesive ● Craft knife ● Self-adhesive aluminum foil ● Hammer ● Upholstery nails ● Gloss medium or clear varnish ● Paintbrush ● 2 hinges (with 4 small screws for each) ● Small screwdriver ● Glue gun ● Thumbtacks.

METHOD

To make the money-covered chest, clean and lightly sand the box to remove any splinters that could pierce the bills.

Working on one side of the box at a time, spray the whole surface with adhesive, then stick the bills in position, overlapping them so that the whole side is covered. Smooth out bubbles and wrinkles in the bills using your thumb, being careful not to rip the bills. Spray underneath any overlapping edges so that they do not curl up.

Cut the self-adhesive aluminum foil into strips long enough to cover each edge of the box. Fold 8 of them at right angles and use these to cover the bottom and side edges. Fold the remaining strips around the top edges of the box and the edges of the lid.

Apply 3 or 4 coats of gloss medium or clear varnish to the finished surface after it has completely dried. Allow the surface to dry between coats.

Hammer upholstery nails around the edges at regular intervals.

Screw the hinges into position to attach the lid to the box.

To make the coin-covered box, attach strips of self-adhesive foil tape to the edges of the box and lid and hammer in upholstery nails, following the instructions given for the money-covered chest.

Working on one side of the box at a time, line up an assortment of coins in rows to cover the surface. Stick them in position using the glue gun. You can attach drilled coins with a thumbtack through the center but be careful that the thumbtacks don't pass through to the inside of the box. If the box sides are too thin, stick the drilled coins to the surface, then either glue the head of a thumbtack on top or leave the hole visible.

Gift wrapping

PAINTED GIFT BAGS

MATERIALS
**White kraft paper ● Scissors ●
Ruler ● Pencil ● Large and small
paintbrushes ● Bowls ● Silk paint
in various colors ● 3D craft paint
● Double-sided tape ● Craft knife
● Ribbon.**

Method
Cut a rectangle of paper to the
dimensions shown on the template
on page 118.

Lay the paper flat and paint with
silk paint diluted with water. Leave
to dry flat to prevent it distorting.

Draw a motif on what will become
the front panel of the bag, then
paint it with the 3D craft paint
following the manufacturer's
instructions. Leave to dry.

Mark all the the folds of the bag—all
should be folded outward except
the central fold on the side gussets,
which should be folded inward.
Close the bag at the back with a
strip of double-sided tape. Fold the
bottom of the bag and close with
double-sided tape.

Pinch the front and back of the bag
together at the top and fold over
twice, by 1¼ in each time. Using
the craft knife, cut 2 parallel vertical
slits in the center of the top of the
bag, cutting through all the layers.
Slide a length of decorative ribbon
through the slits and tie it in a bow
at the front of the bag.

(see also page 118)

Gift wrapping

MINI SILVER BOXES

MATERIALS
Aluminum foil ● Scissors ● Small metal cake pans ● Beads, fake gems, ribbon ● Strong glue.

METHOD
Cut the aluminum foil into small pieces of matching size. Lay them on top of each other until you have a thickness that holds its shape well but is still pliable (the number of layers you need will depend on the quality of the foil used).

To create the outside of the gift box, cover the outside of the cake pan with these pieces of foil, ensuring that layers adhere to each other. The overlapping of the pieces will give the finished box substance. Cut off any edges of foil that are overhanging the top of the pan, then remove the pan.

Repeat the above steps, this time layering the foil pieces inside the tin, to create the inside of the box. To finish, glue a bead, fake gem, or length of ribbon to the bottom of the inside box.

Gift wrapping

LEAFY ENVELOPES

MATERIALS

White tissue paper ● Brown wrapping paper ● Scissors ● Craft glue ● Card punch ● Twigs ● Leaves ● White spray paint ● Sheets of scrap paper.

METHOD

Wrap up a present in white tissue paper. Cut a piece of brown wrapping paper with a 2 in overlap so that it is large enough to easily enclose the present when it is folded in half.

Depending on the size of the present, stick 2 or 3 sides together with a line of glue. To close remaining sides, punch 2 holes and thread a twig through them.

To decorate the envelope, cover some leaves with white spray paint, leave to dry, and stick onto the envelope. Alternatively, place some sheets of paper over the ends of the envelope and lay the leaves over the middle section, then spray with paint. Carefully remove the leaves.

Gift wrapping

STATIONERY BAGS
Size: 8⅜ x 5⅜ in

MATERIALS
Large sheets of handwritten paper, ideally aged; if necessary, enlarged on a photocopier ● Medium-thickness iron-on fabric stiffener (the same dimensions as the sheets of paper) ● Ruler ● Pencil ● Scissors ● Sewing machine ● Sewing thread ● Pins.

METHOD
Iron the fabric stiffener to the back of the sheets of paper. Following the template on page 119, draw the shape of the bag and the 2 handles on the back, and cut them out.

Form the bag by folding up the sides, with wrong sides facing, and machine-stitch them together, ⅛ in in from the edges. Stitch all around the base of the bag to define the edges.

Stitch along the lengths of the handles, ⅛ in from the edges. Pin the ends of one handle inside the bag, approximately 3⅝ in apart and equidistant from the sides. Repeat with the other handle on the opposite side. Stitch around the top of the bag, catching the handles into the seam. Remove pins.

To make the bag charms, cut long strips of paper and, with wet fingers, roll them around lengths of cotton thread. Cut out 2 hearts from the handwritten paper and 2 from the fabric stiffener. Lay them on top of each other, slip the end of a twisted paper ribbon between the 2, then iron to adhere the layers together and trap the ribbon.

(see also page 119)

Christmas

ORIENTAL LIDDED BOWLS

MATERIALS

Bowl ● Wallpaper paste ● 2 small round balloons ● String ● Scissors ● 2 large sheets of red paper ● Newspaper ● Pin ● Tape measure ● Pencil ● Craft knife ● Corrugated card (⅝ in-wide strip the length of the perimeter of the papier mâché balloon for each bowl, plus a 2 ⅜ in-diameter circle for the small bowl) ● Strong glue ● Gold-colored wire ● Wire cutters ● Copper-colored multi-surface 3D pen ● 2 decorative beads.

METHOD

In a bowl, prepare the wallpaper paste, following the manufacturer's instructions. Leave to rest for 10 minutes. Blow up the 2 balloons, knot the ends, and tie a piece of string to each from which to suspend them.

Tear the red paper into small pieces. Soak them in the wallpaper paste and then stick them to the balloons until each is covered. Leave to dry overnight.

Repeat, this time using newspaper. Apply a total of 6 or 7 layers of newspaper, allowing each of the first 3 coats to dry before applying the next. Successive layers can be applied 2 at a time. Leave to dry. Finish with a final layer of red paper. Leave to dry again.

Burst the balloon by sticking a pin into the top. Measure the papier mâché balloon to find the center, then draw a straight line in pencil all around the middle. Cut the shape open along this line, using a craft knife. Remove the burst balloon.

For the large bowl, cut a strip of corrugated card ⅝ in wide and the length of the perimeter of the balloon. Glue it to the outside rim of the half that will form the base.

To make the feet for the large bowl, cut 3 lengths of the gold-colored wire, each about 10 in long. Curl one end of a wire into a snail shape and position the other end against the bowl, bending it so that it follows the shape of the bowl from just below the card rim to the base. Attach the wire in place with a line of glue and small pieces of red paper soaked in wallpaper paste. Repeat with the other 2 lengths of wire, placing them equidistant from each other.

Cover the edges and the part of the legs that is attached to the bowl with more wallpaper paste-coated red paper. Leave to dry.

Decorate the rim of the bowl with the copper-colored multi-surface 3D pen. Leave to dry.

Attach a decorative bead to the top of the lid with a drop of glue, and add some motifs using the copper 3D pen.

The small bowl is made in the same way as the large one, but the feet are replaced with a circle of corrugated card, and 2 curled-wire handles are attached to the sides (see opposite).

Christmas

CARDBOARD CHRISTMAS TREE
Size: approximately 5 ft tall

MATERIALS

2 large recycled cardboard boxes (each at least 5 x 3 ½ ft) ● Ruler ● Pencil ● Craft knife ● Scissors ● Double-sided tape ● 2 in-wide gummed kraft paper tape ● Small bowl ● Acrylic paint: 17 fl oz white, 8½ fl oz mid brown ● 2 in- and ¾ in-wide paintbrushes.

METHOD

Divide the cardboard into 4 in squares. Using the templates on pages 120–1, draw the tree shapes using the grid as a guideline. Don't forget to mark the positions for the cardboard wedges.

Cut strips of cardboard about 1 ¼ in wide and to the height of each of the squares marked on the tree shapes. Using double-sided tape, stick them side by side, end on, to one of the tree shapes, in the places indicated, to create wedges and give some thickness to the tree. Stick the duplicate tree on top. Repeat with the other tree shape. Using a craft knife, cut open the slits as shown, adjusting their width to correspond with the thickness of the trees.

To seal the open edges, stick the gummed kraft paper tape around all edges of both trees, including the edges of the slits.

In the small bowl, mix together equal quantities of white and mid-brown acrylic paint and add a small amount of water. Using the wide brush, paint one side of each tree. Leave the trees to dry flat, then turn them over and paint the other side. When they are dry, prop them upright and paint the edges and borders of the shapes with white acrylic paint, using the ¾ in-wide paintbrush.

Slot the 2 tree shapes together.

(see also pages 120–1)

Christmas

FESTIVE WINDOWS

MATERIALS

**Large sheet of red cardstock ●
Carbon paper ● Ballpoint pen ●
Cutting mat ● Craft knife with fine
blade ● Newspaper ● Spray
adhesive.**

METHOD

Enlarge the templates on page 122
on a photocopier, adjusting the size
as necessary to fit your windows.
Place the photocopies onto the red
cardstock, slide the carbon paper
between the 2 layers, then trace
over around the shapes using a
ballpoint pen.

Place the cardstock onto the
cutting mat and, using the craft
knife with a fine blade, carefully cut
out the shapes.

Make sure your windows are clean
and dry before mounting your
window decorations. Place each
decoration on a newspaper-
covered surface and spray with the
spray adhesive, then position on
the window.

(see also page 122)

Christmas

FEATHERS AND STARS

MOBILE

MATERIALS
White wire ● Wire cutters ● A large assortment of white paper ● Craft knife and/or scissors ● Nylon thread ● Strong glue ● White feathers.

METHOD
Curl a length of wire to form the desired shape of the mobile, starting and finishing with a loop. Cut a large number of different snowflake shapes from the white papers and attach them to the wire structure either with short lengths of nylon thread or by gluing them directly to the wire. Intersperse the snowflakes with the white feathers, attaching them in the same way. If the snowflakes and feathers are too heavy and cause the wire shape to uncurl, tie the loops of wire together with lengths of nylon thread.

GLASSES

MATERIALS
White self-adhesive vinyl contact paper ● Carbon paper ● Ballpoint pen ● 6 wine glasses ● Scissors.

METHOD
Enlarge the motif below on a photocopier, then lay the pattern onto the paper backing of the self-adhesive vinyl contact paper, slip a sheet of carbon paper between the 2 layers, and trace over the motif using the ballpoint pen. Repeat until you have traced 6 motifs.

Cut out the motifs, peel off the paper backing, and carefully stick one around the bottom of each wine glass, smoothing out any air bubbles with your fingers before pressing the plastic firmly in place. You can add other smaller motifs above this one, varying them to personalize each glass: hearts, triangles, stars, spots.

2 in

Christmas

PRICKED AND EMBOSSED STATIONERY

PRICKED STATIONERY

MATERIALS
Graph paper ● Thin cardstock and envelopes ● Corrugated card ● Large pointed needle.

METHOD
Select motifs from a cross-stitch book or design your own on graph paper. (Reduce the design on a photocopier to obtain squares of approximately ⅛ in.)
Lay the paper template onto your cardstock or envelope, then place both onto the smooth surface of a piece of corrugated card. Using a large pointed needle, prick each square of the motif to transfer it to the paper.

EMBOSSED STATIONERY

MATERIALS
Brass or plastic letter stencils ● Double-sided tape ● Letter or kraft paper and envelopes ● Embossing tool.

METHOD
Tape the stencil in working position on a hard work surface with double-sided tape. Lay your chosen paper over the top, and with the embossing tool, trace around the edges of the shapes, using the fine point for small areas and the large for big areas.
(This is the same technique as used by childen when they place a piece of paper over a coin and draw over the top with a pencil, for example, only here the pencil is replaced with a hard object.)

Christmas

STORYBOOK BOX
Size: 1⅝ x 8¾ x 6 in

MATERIALS
Metal ruler ● Pencil ● Craft knife ● Thick cardstock ● Stiff cardboard ● Newspaper ● Spray adhesive ● Modern Options gold metallic surfacer ● Modern Options patina blue antiquing solution ● Paintbrush ● Carbon paper ● Gold paint ● Scissors ● White corrugated card ● Tea bag ● Glue gun.

METHOD
Cut a rectangle of 14½ x 8¾ in from the thick cardstock and 2 rectangles of 8¾ x 5⅝ in from the stiff cardboard.

Working on a newspaper-covered surface, cover one side of each of the cardboard rectangles with spray adhesive, then lay the large cardstock rectangle flat and stick the 2 glued pieces at either end as shown on the diagram on page 123 (1).

Paint the whole surface with the gold metallic surfacer. Leave to dry for 1 hour, then apply a second coat. While the paint is still tacky, apply the antiquing solution irregularly over the surface using a paintbrush. Leave to dry: the patina effect will become apparent as the solution dries.

Reduce the template "Secrets" on page 123 and transfer it to the righthand side of the surface by placing a piece of carbon between the template and the cardstock and tracing over the design. Paint over all parts of the design using the gold paint. Leave to dry.

Turn over (so that "Secrets" is face down on the left) and paint this surface gold.

Cut 1 strip of 8 x 1⅝ in and 2 of 6 x 1⅝ in from the remaining stiff cardboard. Round off one end of each of the 2 shorter strips. Using these strips as templates, cut out the same in the corrugated card, positioning the templates so that the grooves run the length of each corrugated-card strip.

Soak the tea bag in a small amount of hot water, allow to cool, then paint the tea over the corrugated card strips to "age" them. Leave to dry, then stick these strips to the cardstock ones using the spray adhesive.

Following the diagram on page 123, mark the inside surface of the box form on the righthand side. Using a glue gun, stick the edges of the card strips in position as shown (2). Leave to dry.

Apply glue to the rounded edges. Fold over the "spine" of the "book" and stick to the edges. The free part will form the lid of the box.

To simulate a leather binding, cut 4 strips of 3⅝ x ⅝ in from the remaining cardstock. Paint them gold, allow to dry, then glue around the spine equidistant from each other.

(see also page 123)

Christmas

RICE-PAPER HEARTS

MATERIALS
Rice-paper rounds (available from an Asian food store) or wafer paper ● Thin card ● Pencil ● Craft knife ● Scissors ● Hole punch ● Ribbon.

METHOD
Lay a rice paper round onto the card and carefully draw round the edge. Draw a heart in the middle of the card circle and, using the craft knife, cut it out to make a template. Place the heart template onto a rice-paper round and draw round the edge with a pencil.

Using the craft knife, make a small cut in the pencil line, large enough to insert the scissors, then carefully cut out the heart. Repeat to obtain several hearts and rounds with hearts removed.

Punch a hole in the top of each shape and thread through a length of ribbon by which to suspend the decoration.

Christmas

WHITE-LEAF MIRROR

MATERIALS
**Mirror ● White tissue paper ●
Repositionable spray adhesive ●
Scissors ● Pencil ● Cardboard
box (optional, see method).**

METHOD
Enlarge the templates opposite on a photocopier and transfer them to the tissue paper. Adjust the number and their sizes, or hand-draw your own, depending on the size of your mirror. Cut out the motifs: the thinness of the tissue paper will enable you to cut through several layers at the same time.

Spray the adhesive onto the back of each motif (ideally spraying outdoors or inside a cardboard box to limit fumes and to prevent adhesive getting onto other surfaces). Stick the shapes carefully onto the mirror, one at a time, beginning with their stems.

To give some relief to the design, cut out the centers of the leaves (shown in gray on the templates) before spraying them with adhesive, or add a thin strip of paper to the center of each leaf.

2 in

Christmas

MANTLEPIECE MAGIC

MATERIALS

Pencil ● Corrugated card ● Craft knife ● Newspaper ● Spray paint: copper, gold, and silver ● Double-sided tape ● Red acrylic paint ● Paintbrush.

METHOD

Draw holly leaves and stars of different sizes and shapes onto the smooth surface of the corrugated card. Vary the position of the motifs so that the grooves of the card run in different directions. Cut out the shapes and remove the central "vein" from the leaves.

Working on a newspaper-covered surface, spray the grooved surface of the shapes with metallic paint. Leave to dry.

Stick a length of double-sided tape to the back of each shape, then stick them around the mantlepiece, mixing up the shapes, colors, and direction of the grooves.

Paint the smooth side of some corrugated card with the red acrylic paint and leave to dry. Cut out some "berries" and attach in the same way between the leaves.

Christmas

LITTLE ANGELS

MATERIALS

Aluminum foil ● Wooden toothpicks ● Tapestry needle ● Glue ● White feathers (2 for each angel) ● Mini fluted tart pan.

METHOD

Tightly scrunch up a piece of aluminum foil into a ball to form the head and another into a cone shape for the body. Join them together by poking the ends of a wooden toothpick into the 2 parts. To make the arms and legs, tightly roll long, thin sausage shapes from aluminum foil, adding extra to one end of each length to form the hands and feet.

Pierce holes in the body with the large needle and slide the arms and legs into them. Hold in place by scrunching the foil on the body around them or glue the ends in place. Insert the feathers into the back in the same way.

To make the hat, line the mini fluted tart pan with 2 or 3 layers of aluminum foil, pressing it into all the grooves. Trim the edges. Remove the foil hat from the tray and place it on the angel's head.

Christmas

TEDDY BEARS

PAPIER MÂCHÉ BEAR

MATERIALS
Newspaper ● Gummed kraft paper tape ● Brown and navy blue kraft paper ● Wallpaper paste ● Bowl ● Stiff cardboard ● Scissors ● Raffia ● Needles ● Sewing thread ● 2 buttons ● Felt-tip pens.

METHOD
Crumple sheets of newspaper into a ball for the head. Make a larger ball for the body and 4 sausage shapes for the arms and legs. Assemble these elements using the gummed kraft paper tape to give you the basic form of the bear.

Tear up strips of the kraft paper, keeping the colors separate. Mix up the wallpaper paste in a bowl, following the manufacturer's instructions. Soak the paper in the wallpaper paste and stick the pieces onto the shape, smoothing out air bubbles. Leave the shape to dry overnight in a warm, dry place.

(continues on page 124)

Christmas

PRECIOUS PICTURES

MATERIALS

Metal ruler ● Pencil ● Stiff cardboard ● Cutting mat ● Craft knife ● Newspaper ● White glue ● Glue brush ● Sandpaper ● Paintbrushes ● White acrylic paint ● Colored inks: jewel colors plus gold.

1. Draw the outlines of the picture frame onto the cardboard. Lay the cardboard onto the cutting mat and cut out the shapes using the craft knife and metal ruler.

2. Tear strips of newspaper and coat them with the white glue. Stick them to the cardboard frame, covering all surfaces with at least 4 layers of paper. Leave to dry.

3. Sand the frame, then paint with the white acrylic paint. Leave to dry for 2 hours, then sand again. Apply a further 2 coats of paint, allowing each to dry for 2 hours and sanding the frame before applying the next.

4. Paint all surfaces with colored ink. Leave to dry. Paint the inner and outer edges of the frame with gold ink. Using your finger, apply small touches of gold ink elsewhere on the frame.

Christmas

SILVER BASKETWEAVE BAG
Size: 3¼ x 5⅝ in

MATERIALS
Aluminum foil ● White rice paper ● White letter paper ● Scissors ● Paper glue ● Ruler ● Pencil ● Adhesive tape.

METHOD
Cut 11 strips of 11 x 1¼ in and 28 strips of 8½ x 1¼ in from the aluminum foil. Cut 10 strips of 11 x 1¼ in from the white rice paper.

Fold each of the strips in 3 lengthwise so that they are each ⅜ in wide. Place a sheet of white letter paper vertically on the work surface, then stick the ends of the 11 in-long strips across bottom, using the paper glue, alternating the foil and rice paper strips. Weave the 28 shorter strips of aluminum foil over and under between these strips to cover the paper. Glue the loose ends of the strips to the sheet of paper.

On the wrong side of the paper, fold the paper 1 in from each width edge and 3⅜ in from each lengthwise edge. Unfold and the paper should look like the diagram on page 125.

Cut along the solid lines to create the gusset. Fold in B, bring together A and C to create the side panels of the bag. Glue the overlapped edges together, allow to dry, and then reinforce on the inside with adhesive tape. Repeat for other side.

Cut some strips of aluminum foil and glue them in place inside the bag on either side to form handles.

(see also page 125)

Christmas

LETTERS FROM THE HEART

MATERIALS

Scissors ● White and colored tracing paper ● Pencil ● Metal ruler.

METHOD

Enlarge the templates (1) to the desired size and, for each heart, cut out 2 shapes in 2 different colors of tracing paper. (Note: the piece between the fold and the end of the cut lines must form a square). Fold each shape in half as shown. Draw the cut lines onto the shapes, ensuring that all 6 bands (A–F) are the same width. Cut along the lines. Lay the 2 hearts as shown (2) and weave the bands together as follows: slide F closed (i.e. taking the 2 layers together) between the 2 layers of A, then B closed between the 2 layers of F, and F closed between the 2 layers of C. Slide A closed between the 2 layers of E, then D closed between the 2 layers of A. Slide E closed between the 2 layers of B, then C closed between the 2 layers of E, B closed between the 2 layers of D, and finally D closed between the 2 layers of C.

Christmas

WALLPAPER TREE
Size: approximately 6½ ft tall

MATERIALS
**1 roll of decorative wallpaper ●
Pencil ● Scissors ● Decorative
paper or paints and paintbrush,
for Christmas ball motifs
(optional, see method) ● Craft
knife ● Styrofoam: 7 rectangles
of $2^3/_4$ x $1^1/_4$ in and 2 rectangles
of 6 x $1^1/_4$ in ● Double-sided tape
● String of mini Christmas lights
● Masking tape.**

METHOD
Draw freehand and then cut out the
4 sections of the Christmas tree:
each should be about 21¼ in tall,
and the width of the top of each
section should correspond to the
base of the one above it.

The "Christmas balls" on the tree
shown opposite are part of the
design of the wallpaper, but if you
are unable to find something similar,
you could use off-cuts from another
decorative paper and stick them in
place on the tree, or simply paint
them onto your chosen wallpaper.
Using the craft knife, cut a small slit
in the center of each "Christmas tree."

Assemble the tree by overlapping
the sections to a greater or lesser
extent depending on the desired
height of the tree. To give the tree a
3D appearance, stick the Styrofoam
rectangles between the 2 layers
using double-sided tape on either
side of the block. (Use one on each
side of the base of the top 2 layers,
3 along the base of the next layer
and the 2 long rectangles at either
side of the base of the tree.)

Beginning at the top of the tree,
slide a mini light into each hole and
tape in place with a piece of
masking tape on the back.

Stick the top of the tree to the wall
using double-sided tape.

Designs and templates

(see page 6)

Some of the templates have been reduced in scale. To find their correct size, enlarge them on a photocopier until the scale bar on the template shows the measurement indicated.

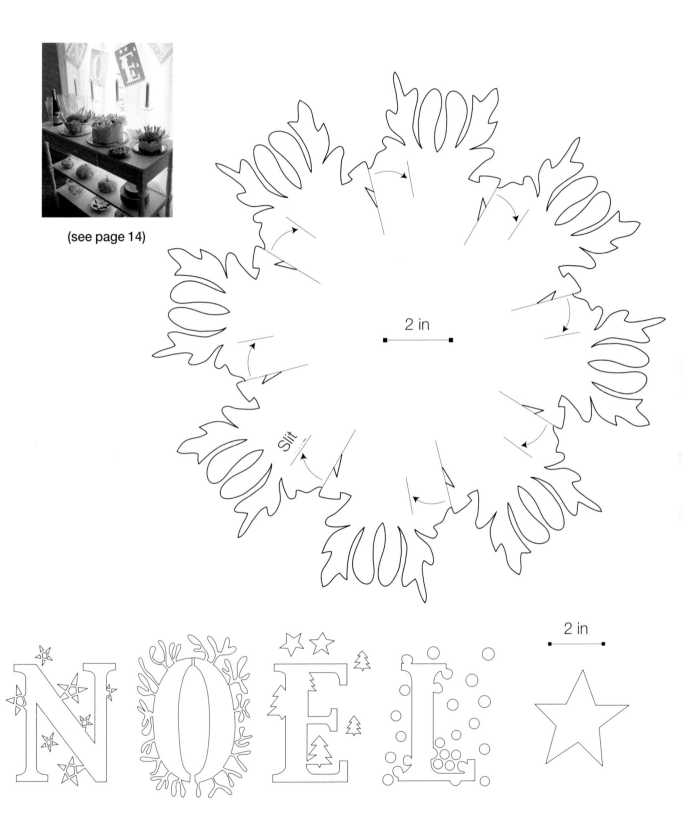

(see page 14)

2 in

2 in

Designs and templates

(see page 24)

1

2

3

4

5

6

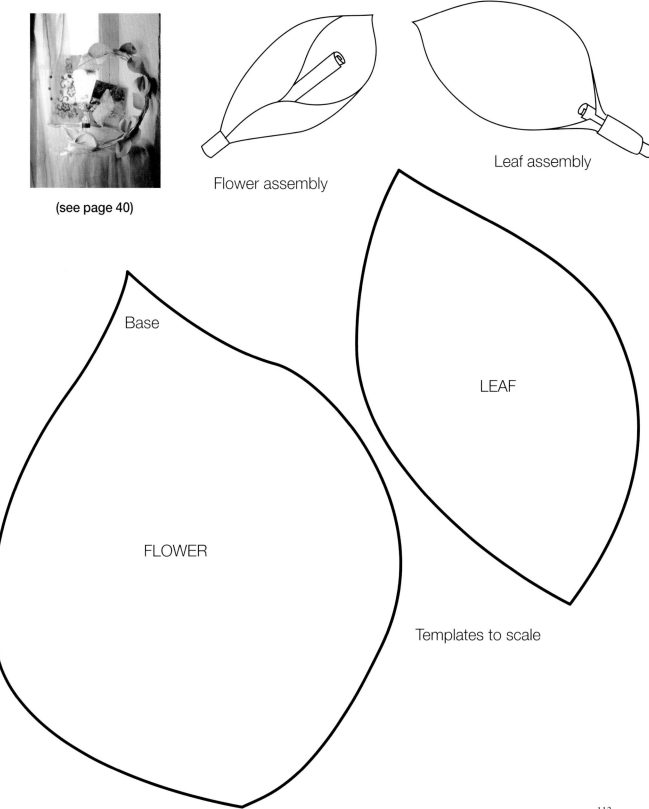

(see page 40)

Flower assembly

Leaf assembly

Base

LEAF

FLOWER

Templates to scale

113

Designs and templates

(see page 42)

Templates to scale

(see page 44)

Designs and templates

(see page 56)

Candle-ring

Arms

Body

2 in

(see page 60)

Wooden rod
↓

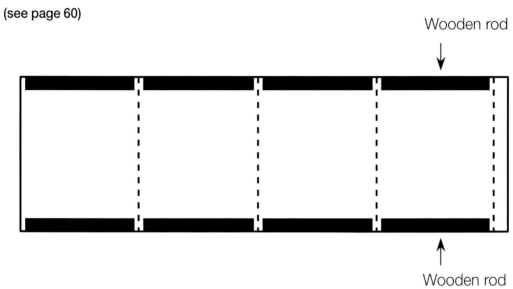

↑
Wooden rod

8 in   8 in   8 in   8 in   ¾ in

12 in

Designs and templates

(see page 72)

Designs and templates

(see page 78)

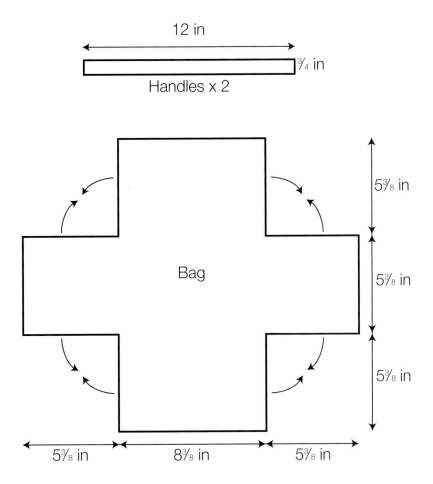

12 in

¾ in

Handles x 2

Bag

5⅜ in

5⅜ in

5⅜ in

5⅜ in

8⅜ in

5⅜ in

Designs and templates

(see page 82)

Cardboard wedges

x 2

Slit: 30 in

1 square = 4 in^2

Slit: 30 in

x 2

1 square = 4 in²

Designs and templates

(see page 84)

4 in

4 in

14½ in

8¾ in

Stiff
cardboard

①

Stiff
cardboard

5⅝ in

6 in

1⅞ in

1⅞ in

②

8 in

5/8 in

3/8 in

(see page 90)

2 in

123

Designs and templates

(continued from page 100)

Rework the form, building it up by adding more paper where needed. When you have achieved the desired shape, cut out the ears from the stiff cardboard. Stick them onto the head with gummed kraft paper tape, then cover them with brown kraft paper coated in the glue. Curve them into shape before they dry. Add a small flattened ball made from crumpled newspaper for the muzzle. Hold it in place with gummed kraft paper.

Cover the whole bear with 6 more layers of glue-soaked paper, the last one brown, allowing each layer to dry before applying the next.

When the bear is completely dry, add the dungarees, using torn strips of glue-coated blue kraft paper. Cut out the shape of the pocket and sew along the edge using the raffia, then stick it in place on the front of the dungarees. Sew a button onto each shoulder strap. Draw on the eyes and snout using the colored felt-tip pens.

TEDDY BEAR TRAY

MATERIALS
Tray ● Colored kraft paper: brown, yellow, white, navy blue, and pale blue ● Paper glue ● Pencil ● Clear varnish ● Paintbrush.

METHOD
Cover the base of the tray with pieces of glue-coated yellow paper, then form a grid by gluing on thin strips of white paper.

Sketch out the shape of the bears in pencil, then glue pieces of colored kraft paper in place to fill the design.

When the glue has completely dried, apply a layer of clear varnish over the whole design to protect the surface.

(see page 104)

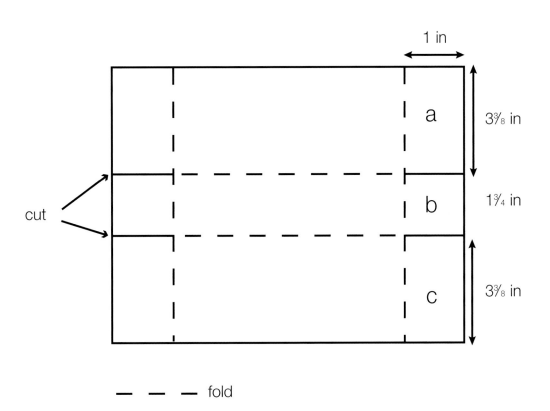

1 in

a   3⅜ in

cut

b   1¾ in

c   3⅜ in

— — — fold

Index

Credits

PHOTOGRAPHERS
Édouard Chauvin (p. 103), Juliette d'Assay (p. 43), Gilles de Chabaneix (pp. 7, 15, 21, 27, 35, 45, 61, 67, 69, 87, 97), Thomas Dhellemmes (pp. 13, 59, 65), Christophe Dugied (pp. 11, 19, 25, 29, 33, 39, 41, 49, 55, 57, 81, 91, 93, 107), Louis Gaillard (pp. 9, 31, 37, 47, 53, 63, 71, 73, 75, 77, 83, 85, 95, 99, 105), Pierre Hussenot (pp. 17, 23, 89), Sylvie Lancrenon (p. 101), Bernard Maltaverne (p. 51), V. Perocheau (p. 109), Frédéric Vasseur (p. 79).

DESIGNERS
Barbro Andersson (p. 107), Marie-France Annasse (p. 13), Nathalie Auzemery (p. 103), Monique Bonnin (pp. 43, 51), Eve-Marie Briolat (pp. 63, 73), Catherine de Chabaneix (pp. 7, 15, 27), Ayako David (p. 67), Ghislaine Descamps (pp. 81, 85, 101), Virginie Desmoulins (pp. 33, 39, 41), Virginie Dillot (pp. 35, 45, 87), Juliette Dupont (p. 47, 59), Céline Dupuy (pp. 25, 77, 83, 95, 109), Marie-Paule Faure (p. 53), Michiru Fujii (pp. 19, 29, 49, 65, 75, 79, 99), Françoise Hamon (pp. 61, 97), Vania Leroy (pp. 9, 11, 55, 71, 91, 105), Véronique Méry (p. 67), Yves Méry (pp. 21, 57), Sonia Richard (p. 23), Évelyne Rouvillois (p. 17), Camille Soulayrol (p. 31), Marion Taslé (pp. 37, 69), Dominique Turbé (p. 93), Laurence Wichegrod (p. 89).

STYLISTS
Ève-Marie Briolat (pp. 63, 73, 109), Pascale Chastres (pp. 23, 31, 89), Catherine de Chabaneix (pp. 21, 35, 45, 61, 67, 69, 87, 97), Virginie Dillot (pp. 7, 15), Christl Exelmans (p. 37), Marie-Paule Faure (p. 53), Marion Faver (pp. 43, 51), Caroline Lancrenon (pp. 23, 89, 101, 103), Vania Leroy (pp. 9, 11, 47, 55, 75, 81, 91, 99, 105), Véronique Méry (p. 27), Camille Soulayrol (pp. 13, 19, 25, 29, 39, 41, 49, 57, 59, 65, 71, 77, 79, 83, 85, 93, 95, 107), Dominique Turbé (pp. 25, 33, 107).